WHOSE NAMES HAVE SLIPPED AWAY

poems by

Kathy Nelson

Finishing Line Press
Georgetown, Kentucky

WHOSE NAMES HAVE SLIPPED AWAY

Copyright © 2017 by Kathy Nelson
ISBN 978-1-63534-106-5 First Edition
All rights reserved under International and Pan-American Copyright Conventions.
No part of this book may be reproduced in any manner whatsoever without written permission from the publisher, except in the case of brief quotations embodied in critical articles and reviews.

ACKNOWLEDGMENTS

The author would like to thank the editors of the publications in which these poems first appeared, some in earlier versions:
Great Smokies Review: "Friends," "I Alone Am Left to Say Your Name," "Fall"
US 1 Worksheets: "Dispossessed," "Sleep Exercise," "Rapunzel"
Edison Literary Review: "The Moose"
The Cortland Review: "The Question"
Wild Goose Poetry Review: "Whether But When"
Kakalak: "Before the Hurricane"
Off the Coast: "Lilly Belle Easterly, age 19, Red River Texas, 1889"
The Quiet Earth: Nature and Health (Massachusetts Audubon Society): "Whose Names Have Slipped Away"
Asheville Poetry Review: "Enough"

Publisher: Leah Maines

Editor: Christen Kincaid

Cover Art: Kathy Nelson

Author Photo: Bruce L. Nelson

Cover Design: Elizabeth Maines

Printed in the USA on acid-free paper.
Order online: www.finishinglinepress.com
also available on amazon.com

Author inquiries and mail orders:
Finishing Line Press
P. O. Box 1626
Georgetown, Kentucky 40324
U. S. A.

Table of Contents

Grenade 1
Conclave 2
Whose Names Have Slipped Away 3
Lilly Belle Easterly, age 19, Red River, Texas, 1889 4
Ice 5
The Question 6
Whether But When 7
Now, the Storm 8
Rapunzel 9
Before the Hurricane 10
Void 11
After Peaches 12
Enough 13
Dispossessed 14
Friends 15
In the Shadow of Notch Mountain 16
Love in Winter 17
The Moose 18
From Mt. Leconte 20
I Alone Am Left to Say Your Name 22
Sleep Exercise 23
Owl 24
Fall 25
The Bright Trees of November Are Speaking 26

*To my parents, Jane and Travis
and to my two daughters, Nora and Fran*

Grenade

We climb, sweat-sticky
    into the tangle of Bois d'Arc branches,
our knees and elbows, our shins scoured
      by deep-rutted bark.
Long thorns hidden among the leaves
    and in the crooks of limbs
could pierce a thigh, gash a forearm, a side.

We weigh the risk.

Neighborhood kids after horse apples.
The great globes hang, green gewgaws
    the color of lime jello,
among deep shadows of leaves.

When we reach them, we rip them from their stems,
    heave them like hand grenades
onto the driveway.
Too green, they bounce in the yard;
    at perfect ripeness, they shatter
      into an oozing mass.
Or we impale them on thorns,
    watch their sticky white milk.

After the others have gone home, after
    I have shoveled the mess
under my mother's harsh eye
    I find red in the white rectangle
of my underwear. The first.
I do not show my mother. I tell no one.

Conclave

Three large turtles bask on the bank of the lagoon,
two of them still gleam with dark water.

A fourth climbs slowly up to sun, the yellow markings of his underside
lifted as he works his body, one grass-flattening flipper at a time.

A crawl of turtles.

They stretch their black heads up and out toward the sun.

A heliotrope of turtles.

Yesterday, eighteen egrets roosted, slender white sigmoids
blending into palm shadows.
I searched a word for the collection: a flight, a deliberation.

Now, five large turtles bask.
A congregation.

Three more, black heads raised above the water,
approach through floating algae.

A stealth.

A harbor.

Suddenly, the plop of bodies.
A neighbor with his camera clomps down his stairs.

An emptiness of turtles.

But soon, they clamber back, others swimming slowly in,
shadows in dark water.

An armada.

Whose Names Have Slipped Away

The sun one thumb's length above the farthest trees,
I walk the morning road, the soft dirt tracked
by heavy tires, shaded by the fringed mimosa,
scarlet oak, tulip poplar, others.

Shadows stretch from sunlit stones
and Queen Anne's lace leans along the fence.
A robin drops down,
sudden raptor to a rattling June bug,
and in the field hay bales bask beside the baler.

Six black cows dip their heads
into grass, chewing, lashing their tails,
and from the house next to the field a rooster
calls out clear and high, and trellised grapevines
climb like lines of new recruits over the hill.

I've come out to find my bearings.

I am the child of ones who walked.
And even though their road was dust
and their trees scrub cedars,
their flowers thistles, nettles, cattails,
and hawks ravaged hapless squirrels,
and red cows scrabbled among burr-grass,

and even though they walked their road
to harvest cotton fields that promised
hands would bleed and backs would ache,
still it is their road I walk,
looking for landmarks, signposts.

Lilly Belle Easterly, age 19, Red River, Texas, 1889

Dear Despair,
I wake again from the watery dream—
cascades in a canyon of rock, my body
billowing among the boulders, and I cannot see shore.
Two weeks ago, we ferried across the Mississippi,
and I'll not see my mama anymore.

Dear Desolation,
the stars begin to fade
and in the east, the sun takes up again
its searing purpose. I have told my husband
I will go no farther. The child grows heavy
in my belly and the mule is lame.

There is nothing here of home, no slow Nolachucky
flows along the Appalachians, green
under elms and chestnuts. Only this brown gully,
these wide prairies, and what my mama gave me
while she wiped her tears and could not speak:

A Dutch oven, seasoned with the fat of two hogs.
Recipes written in her hand.
A bolt of gingham. Needles. Scissors.
A butter mold my father made.
Ten pounds of flour milled from the field.
A pound each—salt and sugar—three of coffee.
The planes my grandpa used to build the house
there where the river bends,
the timbers smoothed by his strong arm.
A Bible, all our names inscribed.

Here there are no cows, no trees tall enough for timber,
among the thistles and mesquite,
oh, Mercy, oh, Refuge.

Ice

Peppers hang like grenades
from stems wrecked by early snow.

The child, her knees bare,
still waits for a word.

A mountain range between us,
still my mother finds me.

Where are you? Why aren't you here?

The long roots of complaint reach deep
into the ground—hers, mine.

On the highway, kudzu holds back
the proximate rock slide.

I hurry to outrun
her angry face, the icy curves.

The Question

I remember the back of my mother's head, her stooped shoulders;
how she looked out the window onto fruit trees,
green lawn, the pond; how she did not turn around
but asked her question with the back of her head.

I remember her voice, balanced somewhere between sad
and indignant, teetering between destitute and imperial;
how the room suddenly held so much that was new;
how she had never asked me before

are you angry with me?;
how I stood in the dark of that room,
my gut as heavy as one of her swirling
Murano paperweights; how I let the silence expand.

I no longer remember what - choked words, slammed spoon—
made her ask, or what I answered, but I remember gray hair,
creases at the back of her neck, her breaking voice,
and the long pause before I opened my mouth.

Whether But When

Mother, it won't stop raining. A gray wall hangs
beyond the nearest trees. Water stands
in emerald grass no one has cut, waiting for a dry day.
Clothes mildew over chairs on the covered porch.
I'll have to wash them again, unworn.
Blighted vines droop in the garden.

Your heart beats like mine, wants what mine wants:
the small white butterflies lighting on the curved fingers
of leaves, the chambered pomegranate, its jewels.

We speak in asides, tell each other nothing.
Time grows short. The paper says the question
is not whether but when this year will break
the rainfall record. All night, the fret of rain.

Now, the Storm

In the dark
the locomotive wind careens
against the red walls of the night

then crashes
in the trees above the house.
Once, this heart beat steady;

now, it gales then stalls,
before the banshee
resumes its howl.

All these years
the tidy chambers
the ordered clockwork.

Rapunzel

A wet towel remains,
    abandoned in a heap,
at the bathroom door.
Bobbie pins strew the sink.
The dryer dangles.
The straightening iron,
    agape.
The smell of singed hair.
Long dark strands drift
across white tile.
Bottles litter the shower floor.

I should have known—
    straight-ahead eyes
across the table,
in the hallway;
    silence brooding
in her room.
Fifteen, she was practicing
    escape.

The little girl who used to ask,
Mommy, braid my hair?
I could have trimmed it
bit by bit, every night
as she slept,
    kept her.

Before the Hurricane

The banister is sticky.
The wild locust quivers,
shivers like a dog's flank.

Plastic jugs of water
stand in rows on the counter,
flashlights wait in the bathroom,
the kitchen, each nightstand.

We leave the windows open
another hour, maybe two.

Two days from twenty-one
our daughter calls: *Mom, can I use
your credit card in the liquor store?*

Six months old,
I held her with one hand
unloading groceries with the other
and all at once she pushed—both legs.

Her body thudded to the floor.
I did not move, waited
for her to breathe.

Outside it's calm
as on that day.
The dogwood stood
silent in the yard.

We were ready.
Then we weren't.

Void

My umbrella streams.
My mother's drips
cold New York November
on my shoulder.
At my knees, water spills
over the black edge
into Inverse Tower One.
Below, a square black pool,
within it, lower still, another,
then another. Water falls—
one pool to the next,
an infinite cascade into darkness.
Black sky above, another void.
Through the crash of water,
the phone chirps. My daughter—
twenty-one, single, pregnant—
pours through cell phone static:

Grandma says I don't deserve my family.

The ground dissolves, rushes
with the rest into the deep.
One generation to the next,
the grief of daughters.

After Peaches

Let it be a good sign:

the quick shadow of hawk
across sunlit peach boughs—

We want the small white
butterflies settling
on the curved leaves

and this communion

clouds floating
over the Swannanoa Mountains.

Too, the inscrutable stonehenge
of squirrel-strewn pits
along the porch railing—

We were so young together once.

The summer scatter
of yellow leaves
among the fallen fruit—

and the peach boughs
unburdened.

Enough

In this heat, a body decomposes fast.
Last week, a squirrel lay dead beside the pool.
The thing we fear consumes us at the last.

My heart sank, thinking of the gruesome task;
but off I went in search of the right tool.
In this heat, a body decomposes fast.

When I returned, I saw, taken aback,
maggots teeming, feeding, heaving. Who'll
deny our fear consumes us at the last?

Later, nothing but a damp, grey mass
no longer recognizable as squirrel.
In this heat, a body decomposes fast.

I looked today (the sky was overcast).
Nothing left but spectral spine, perfect skull.
The thing we feared consumed us at the last.

Perhaps you've had enough of death? you ask.
Enough indulgence in the catacombs? You'll
agree, a body decomposes fast.
What we keep secret often shows up last.

Dispossessed

Cactus, kalanchoe, and cyclamen
shiver in their pots.

Fat and slow,
with markings, colors of a tiger,
a spider clings to sagging silk
between two waxy jade leaves,
stands her ground when I insist—
you may not come into my house—
and crouches closer to the stem,
her eight fierce legs working
her heavy body into shadow.

I reach a finger down
and flick her to the porch
where she lands,
a refugee—nothing
to show for summer's
elegant spinning.
She scuttles,
awkward as a cockroach,
for the closest corner.

That's when I remember.
I know how it goes
when home leaves you:
the sudden scurry for safety,
rage.

Friends

Stepping off the porch, I saw two feet away:
a rag left carelessly, or someone's hat.
My mind refused, relented, finally let in
the looping, muscled form, diamond skin,
the awful sentience centered in the coil.

Along the curving body, rusty rhombs,
their brown rims joining at the spine,
like weathered saddles. Silent
and discrete, the tail was tucked
beneath the sequined sheath.

In stillness, curves looped endlessly
around, narrowing,
reversing, narrowing again—
delicate neck, the wide, flat jaw,
narrowing to arrow. Copperhead.

Big as a dinner plate, she sunned
beside the step; I hugged the farthest
possible edge, watched for movement,
searched for eyes, a glance—*if she'd return
my gaze, we could be friends.*

She dozed or watched, eye slits fixed.
She never moved. For weeks, after she left,
all night her babies swam in the streaming street,
quick six-inch sine waves, lifted heads.
All night, my ungloved hands reached

deep into garden weeds, pulled up
unseen forms. All night her coils unleashed,
propelled that lethal head, those fangs.
And every day I looked for her beside the step,
her absence still there in the flattened grass.

In the Shadow of Notch Mountain

You went on up the trail from Lake Constantine;
the sky lay flat among firs and boulders.
I hiked down alone, got in the car
and drove to where you'd pointed on the map.

Hours went; the sun climbed down
the sky, I imagined fracture,
faulty map, diamondback,
and the sun kept falling down

and down. When it touched the earth
I started up the trail to find you,
never mind it would soon be dark,

and after only fifty feet or so, you were there,
walking toward me, as though my moving
toward you made you move toward me.

Love in Winter

Do you remember
that January up north
when it snowed three feet
and we went out together
into the white?
We each had a shovel
and worked,
side by side,
no words required,
knowing each other;
the muffled
thunder of snow
falling by shovelfuls
was the only sound
besides our breathing
and I unzipped
my jacket and you
took yours off
and even though it was
sixteen degrees,
each of us
was sweating,
and neither of us
could speak.

The Moose

The dog whimpered
to be let out of our tent.
We stuck our heads out
just in time to see
a moose,
seven hundred pounds
of legs and antlers, hooves,
lumber uphill,
our thirteen pound mutt
running full tilt behind.
His terrier heart propelled him,
black nose to the ground,
shoulders grinding up the slope,
into the woods.

The wild had taken him before.
He'd come back porcupined and bleeding,
or bleary, stinking of skunk.
But moose! We feared
this time was the last.

We took our time packing up,
rolled, rerolled the sleeping bags,
made extra coffee, called.

Our rations would not last
an extra day; we hoisted our packs.
All day we walked.
Ten miles on, the sun went down.

An hour after dark, a familiar whine,
a scratch at the zippered tent door.
He came in, refused to eat,
nosed into my sleeping bag,
made half a circle, fell asleep.

He could not say how far he'd gone
or confess the moment he'd given up,
the trail grown cold
or the moose turned mean.
He never said if there were snakes
or how his feet ached
finding us again.

From Mt. Leconte

    I.   The Lodge

A child, I slept,
    safe,
on a pallet
next to my parents' bed.
Christmas wind
against the windows,
gas flame burned blue
across the room.

We have come to this peak because—
    metal hips and knees,
        arrhythmic heart—
it is not yet too late.

November, the blue flames
in the dark,
wind fists the window,
cold seeps
    through stiff wool,
snow instead of sleep.

Four degrees,
    twenty mile an hour wind
three inches of snow,
        a sheen of ice.

II. The Trail

My boot tread slides, then holds.
Only one way down
    out of the cold.

The trail called Boulevard is endless.
Snow weights my boots.
I walk no longer to arrive
but to push the shuddering
    cold away.
Icicles spine the ridge.

Six-toed bear print,
dwarfs my hand.
I trail a big cat's
    three-padded track.
Blue shadows
weight the snow.

Golden feathers flurry across the white–
a wishbone gleams among their red.

Three o'clock light burns horizontal
    through thick pine—
white snow, black trunks, red light.

Darkness takes the trail.
Ice flows over step-downs.

We choose:
a root or a slab
    of icy stone.
The root may break;
The tread may not hold.

I Alone Am Left to Say Your Name

The astronauts walked on the moon.
It all was dust: you were not there.
Sometimes, the year grown long,

I pass the house. The Bois d'Arc's there,
its thorns. The dogwood, gone.
I can't say what I'm looking for—

your brogan boots,
your fishing rod against the car,
your briefcase at the door?

Mother could not bear your books.
She gave them to me, your desk,
every picture. She does not speak of you.

I long to hear: *you are so much
like your father.* I wait in vain.

Sleep Exercise

Think of a dark lake lying flat,
cedars a dark edge
against the water.

Think of cool metal under foot,
the pulse of ripples against
a small boat.

A lantern burning on the bow.
                                    My father

whispers,
reminds me to keep quiet
not to scare the fish.

Think of the small girl, the melody,
her father's stillness, the dark canopy,
the rocking.

Owl

At midnight, along the creek,
an owl calls from the tall trees.

I do not see the owl or know
what kind she is.

I sense her, dark and hulking,
her scouring

for warm blood on the ground.
Her slow song seeps

into the hollows of
my heartbeats, silences

my footsteps; the opossum
stops his plodding.

Perhaps the DNA
we share pricks our ears,

the opossum's and mine,
for the final silence.

Fall

Steep, stark the wall of longing.
Still the deepening valley,
the nameless lost.
Harsh the searing grammar of absence.
The mountains burn.

The Bright Trees of November Are Speaking

Listen.

When the sap is green
and light plays hide and seek
among the beauties,
you are full of projects.
Then, letting go seems hard, unjust, impossible.

It seems it will go on like that forever.

Then, the arc of the sun lowers,
the nights grow longer.
Your gaze turns inward
the sap falling back,
deep into roots.

Brilliance overtakes you—
like a swelling belly
or a seed pod about to open.

The mountains, on fire
with gold, vermilion,
open into the great earth.

Kathy Nelson grew up near the southern Appalachians but lived in many other places—Austin, Salt Lake City, suburban New Jersey—before those mountains called her and her husband back home. She takes delight in the fact that she lives four miles from the Blue Ridge Parkway and that she has native azalea, rhododendron, and mountain laurel growing in her yard.

The music of words has enthralled Kathy from the beginning. Although she has studied many disciplines, including French literature (M.A), Mechanical Engineering (M.S.), and theology (M.Div.), and has worked in widely varying fields, including teaching, telecommunications engineering, and hospice chaplaincy, poetry has been the thread through all of them. She has felt both fed and ignited by the poetry of Jane Hirschfield, Marie Howe, Ellen Bryant Voigt, Wendell Berry, Tina Barr and many others. Like many poets, Kathy finds that writing is a way of integrating and understanding her experience and is, therefore, essential.

Kathy is grateful for the inspiration and nourishment she has received from poetry writing groups in NJ and NC, as well as from programs like the Great Smokies Writing Program (Asheville) and the Fine Arts Work Center (Provincetown).

www.ingramcontent.com/pod-product-compliance
Lightning Source LLC
LaVergne TN
LVHW041518070426
835507LV00012B/1657